CREATURES OF THE CRETACEOUS

by Louise Nelson

Minneapolis, Minnesota

Credits: All images are courtesy of Shutterstock.com, unless otherwise specified. With thanks to Getty Images, Thinkstock Photo, and iStockphoto. Cover – Warpaint, Konstantin G, Julia-art, Nikulina Tatiana, Zdenek Klucka. Images used on every page – Julia-art, Wetzkaz Graphics, Nikulina Tatiana, Zdenek Klucka. 2 – Warpaint. 4–5 – Catmando, Dotted Yeti, Orla. 6–7 – Herschel Hoffmeyer, Viktorya170377. 8–9 – Herschel Hoffmeyer, Martin Weber. 10–11 – Michael Rosskothen, Warpaint. 12–13 – Daniel Eskridge, Michael Rosskothen. 14–15 – Catmando. 16–17 – Daniel Eskridge, Dotted Yeti, Martin Pelanek. 18–19 – Daniel Eskridge, James Wagstaff. 20–21 – Mark_Kostich, paleontologist natural. 22–23 – Ekaterina Verbis, Warpaint.

Library of Congress Cataloging-in-Publication Data is available at www.loc.gov or upon request from the publisher.

ISBN: 979-8-88509-363-7 (hardcover)
ISBN: 979-8-88509-485-6 (paperback)
ISBN: 979-8-88509-600-3 (ebook)

© 2023 Booklife Publishing
This edition is published by arrangement with Booklife Publishing.

North American adaptations © 2023 Bearport Publishing Company. All rights reserved. No part of this publication may be reproduced in whole or in part, stored in any retrieval system, or transmitted in any form or by any means, electronic, mechanical, photocopying, recording, or otherwise, without written permission from the publisher.

For more information, write to Bearport Publishing, 5357 Penn Avenue South, Minneapolis, MN 55419.

CONTENTS

The Time of Dinosaurs 4
The Cretaceous Period 6
Dinosaurs of the Cretaceous 8
Not a Dino. 10
How Do We Know? 12
Quetzalcoatlus 14
Kronosaurus. 16
Kaprosuchus 18
Mosasaurus 20
End of the Cretaceous. 22
Glossary 24
Index 24

THE TIME OF DINOSAURS

Triassic

Long, long ago, very different creatures wandered Earth. Some had big bodies, terrifying teeth, or terrific tails. They were dinosaurs!

Dinosaurs lived on our **planet** for about 165 million years. This part of the past is known as the Mesozoic Era. It includes the Triassic, Jurassic, and Cretaceous periods.

Jurassic

Cretaceous

There were different dinos during different periods.

THE CRETACEOUS PERIOD

Check out how Earth looked during the Cretaceous!

The Cretaceous period went from 145 to 66 million years ago. At this time, Earth's **continents** were changing. They started to spread farther apart.

Earth was warmer at the beginning of the Cretaceous. However, it cooled down over this time. Flowering plants first showed up as Earth changed.

DINOSAURS OF THE CRETACEOUS

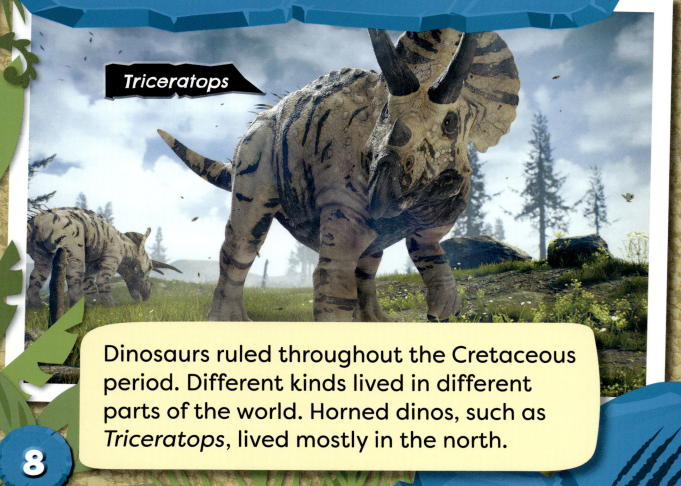

Triceratops

Dinosaurs ruled throughout the Cretaceous period. Different kinds lived in different parts of the world. Horned dinos, such as *Triceratops*, lived mostly in the north.

NOT A DINO

Many dinosaurs lived during the Cretaceous period. But other creatures did, too.

Dinosaurs are a specific group of animals. All dinosaurs are **reptiles**. Their legs come out from right under their bodies.

But not all reptiles are dinos. Non-dino reptiles have legs that come out from the sides of their bodies.

HOW DO WE KNOW?

How can we tell who was a dino? We look at what the animals left behind. Scientists called **paleontologists** (*pale*-ee-uhn-TOL-uh-jists) study these ancient creatures.

Old bones called fossils can help them understand what happened in the past. Paleontologists can learn what a creature might have looked like or how it may have acted.

Whose bones have we found?

Quetzalcoatlus was big and scary. But it was NOT a dinosaur.

A Quick Look

Flying Giraffe
Quetzalcoatlus was as tall as a giraffe. It was one of the largest flying animals of all time.

Meat Eater
This big beast chowed down on small dinosaurs and fish.

Plane Wings
Quetzalcoatlus' wings spread out wider than those of a small plane.

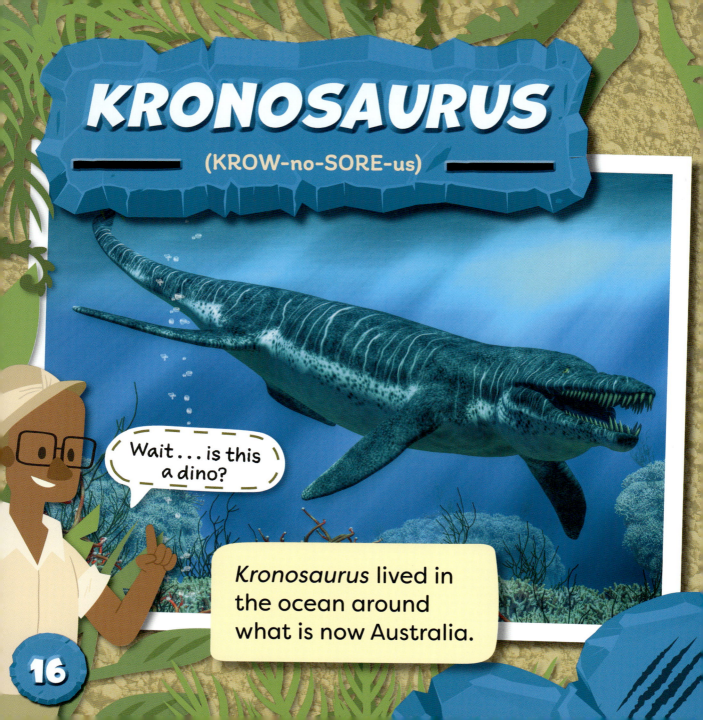

A Quick Look

Godly Name
Kronosaurus was named after a Greek god.

Meat Eater
This swimming predator ate other sea creatures.

Crocodile Jaws
Kronosaurus opened its jaws wide like a crocodile.

This creature was NOT a dinosaur.

A Quick Look

Tusky Crocodile
Kaprosuchus was a bit like a crocodile with big tusks.

Meat Eater
This creature's large, razor-sharp teeth chomped through other animals with ease.

Traveler
Kaprosuchus walked long distances on land.

Don't let the big teeth fool you. This was NOT a dinosaur.

A Quick Look

Long Body
Mosasaurus was huge! This giant was longer than a school bus.

Meat Eater
This swimming predator ate other large creatures.

Living Relatives?
The modern monitor lizard is related to Mosasaurus.

This big beast was NOT a dinosaur.

Monitor lizard

END OF THE CRETACEOUS

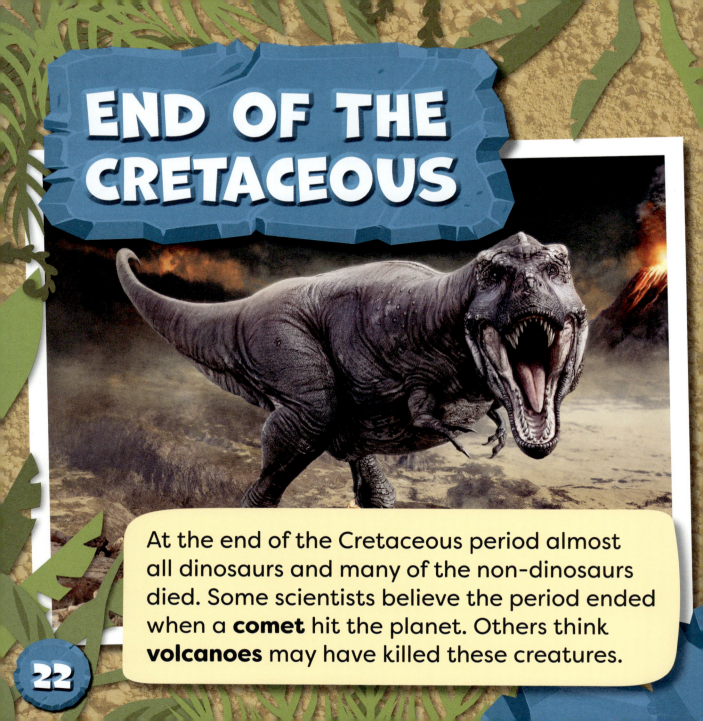

At the end of the Cretaceous period almost all dinosaurs and many of the non-dinosaurs died. Some scientists believe the period ended when a **comet** hit the planet. Others think **volcanoes** may have killed these creatures.

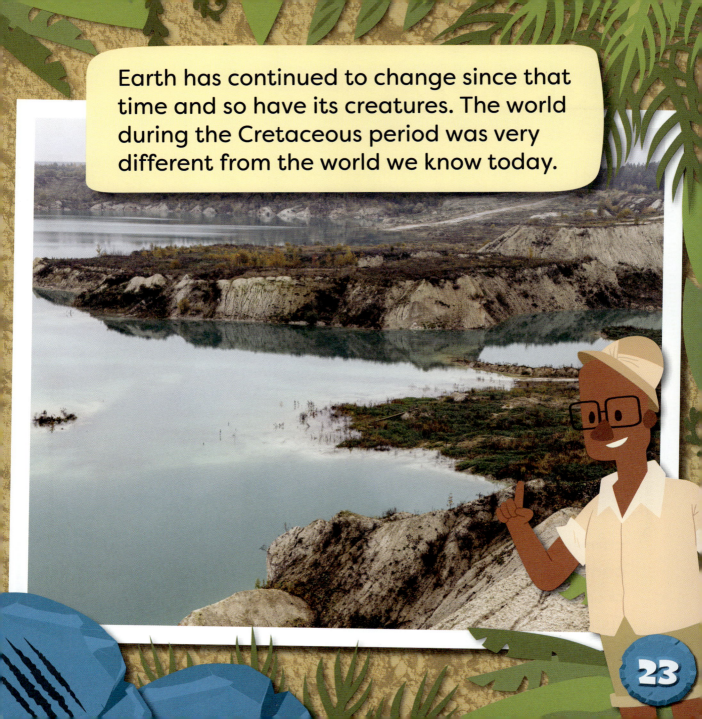

Earth has continued to change since that time and so have its creatures. The world during the Cretaceous period was very different from the world we know today.

GLOSSARY

comet a flying object that comes from space and may strike a planet

continents the world's seven large land masses

paleontologists scientists who study fossils to find out about life in the past

planet a large, round object that circles the sun or another star

predator an animal that hunts and kills other animals for food

reptiles cold-blooded animals that breathe air and have scaly skin

skull the bones of the head

volcanoes mountains that can send out rocks, ash, and lava in sudden explosions

INDEX

comet 22
continents 6
crocodiles 17, 19
fish 15
fossils 13
Mesozoic Era 5
paleontologists 12–13, 18
reptiles 10–11, 20
Triassic period 4–5
Triceratops 8–9
Tyrannosaurus rex 9